I0821519

The Essential Robert Gibbs

The Essential Robert Gibbs

selected by Brian Bartlett

The Porcupine's Quill

Library and Archives Canada Cataloguing in Publication

Gibbs, Robert, 1930–
[Poems. Selections]
The essential Robert Gibbs / selected by Brian Bartlett.

(Essential poets ; 8)
Includes bibliographical references.
ISBN 978-0-88984-349-3

I. Bartlett, Brian, 1953– II. Title.
III. Series: Essential poets (Erin, Ont.) ; 8.

PS8563.I25A6 2012 C811'.54 C2011-908084-2

1 2 3 • 14 13 12

Published by The Porcupine's Quill, 68 Main Street, PO Box 160, Erin, Ontario N0B 1T0. http://porcupinesquill.ca

The poems from *Driving to Our Edge* are reprinted with the permission of Oberon Press.

Represented in Canada by the Literary Press Group.
Trade orders are available from University of Toronto Press.

We acknowledge the support of the Ontario Arts Council and the Canada Council for the Arts for our publishing program. The financial support of the Government of Canada through the Canada Book Fund is also gratefully acknowledged.

Table of Contents

Foreword

The word 'grace' suggests swans, gazelles or wildcats, but look at what Robert Gibbs does with it: 'My poems should have the grace / to hop off the page / like the frog in the Scotchman's porridge / as clean as they came'. Here a key recurring word in Gibbs's poetry, 'grace', gets combined with a metaphorical wit characteristic of him. You would be a sleepy reader to explore his lines for very long before discovering their playfulness. He is drawn to kennings ('puddingstone', 'shadowgraphs', 'springsongs'), puns and homonyms ('unread herring', 'prince of whales', 'damned river dammers'), and other sorts of doublings and echoes ('unhollowed / hallowed', 'my dotage my / anecdotage', 'amphoric euphoria'). 'A Post-Christmas Carol' delivers sombre images of war, hunger and cold, yet the poem's language is complicated and leavened with a description of camels as 'snooty' and a reference to 'Guernica's broken critters' (Picasso's figures are horrific in fragmentation, yet 'critters' is tonally different from 'beasts' or 'creatures'). In his eight books of poetry Gibbs is never lugubrious, and he plumbs depths of insight and imagination with an attractive mixture of the casual and the polished, the idiomatic and the freshly turned. The verbal dexterity of his poems is suggested by the title of his new and selected poems of 1985, *The Tongue Still Dances*.

The uniqueness of this poetry arises from many elements besides verbal sportiveness. Gibbs's book titles *The Road from Here* and *Driving to Our Edge* belong to a motif of voyaging; poems not included in this selection, such as the long, multi-part train-trip 'Six-stage Crossing', 'The Pines of Route 7', and one of his finest expansive poetic achievements, 'The Perpetuation of Worlds Knowledge Has Disproven', turn journeys through space into journeys through perception and understanding. A strong attachment to earthly imagery is signalled by his book titles *Earth Charms Heard So Early* and *Earth Aches* (titles belonging to a pattern in Atlantic Canadian literature including Charles G.D. Roberts' *Earth's Enigmas*, Alden Nowlan's *A Darkness in the Earth*, M. Travis Lane's *Touch Earth*, and Don Domanski's *Earthly Pages*). Overlappings between day and night, the unconscious and the conscious, are touched on in the titles *A Dog in a Dream*, *All This*

Night Long, and *A Kind of Wakefulness*. For hints of a religious sensibility – a sense of the good and the sacred – underlying his writing, we can turn to titles of his books of fiction *A Mouthorgan for Angels*, *Angels Watch Do Keep*, and *Kindly Light*, but that sensibility is very significant in the poetry as well.

Gibbs combines the sensuous – 'all this green liquefaction', 'blueberries bluest fat and thick' – and the metaphysical; this is a poetry not afraid of saying things like 'The Primal / is what we're after', or of asking questions that may be unanswerable: 'Does love this love / concentrate or dissipate?'; 'Why / did the sky blacken again without / intention?'; 'Who asked me to be a reader / of entrails...?'. Much of Gibbs's poetry is understated – though it's too precise and original to be considered merely plain-speaking – so when he does write with explicit intensity in a metaphysical vein, the results are arresting:

> If I could split free
> of forethought and afterthought
> I'd make lawless noises
>
> of love with no measures
> taking out stitches
> of all that seems seamed ...

Even here the abstractness of escapes from thought into 'lawless' expressions is immediately followed by the word-play of 'seems seamed', imagery of brides measuring veils 'like daisies sighted in tall timothy', and the specific time-frame of St. Lucie's Day. Gibbs's writing about grace, love and freedom brings us closer to the quotidian, the seasonal and the bodily rather than away from them.

His poems are often immersed in New Brunswick landscapes or reflect his years in his beloved native city of Saint John – citing places like Smuggler's Cove, Indiantown, Partridge Island and Beulah Campground – and his adopted city of Fredericton. As the author of several books of fiction rooted in vivid personalities of Saint John in the 1940s, he also colours his poetry with affectionate portraits of people such as his father (an engraver with 'eyeglass wrenched into play'), Aunt May of a 'tight-lipped tribe' and 'suppressed laughter',

Paddy McGaughey dancing a Donegal jig (in a poem I imagine illustrated by young Jack Yeats), and Littlejohn Tow, a Lincolnshire immigrant to New Brunswick.

Gibbs's poetry honours other arts, in its attention to painting or carving, and to music – typically not symphonies or grand pianos, but ukuleles, a fiddle playing 'reels and polkas and old Baptist hymns', his father's cello, or 'Wenceslas's treble-voiced page'. The bedrock of writers influencing Gibbs includes Mother Goose, Lewis Carroll, Dickens, Hopkins and religious texts, in particular the diction and cadences of the Bible, though Gibbs's world also welcomes Chinese koans and Japanese Noh theatre. In a poem that includes the words 'grace', 'saints', and 'mercy', a refusal to 'cut out / a single blade of grass / or feather fallen from one bird' evokes 'He sees the sparrow fall' from the New Testament; and in a section from 'Verse Journal', one of Gibbs's experiments in daily writing, the lines 'breasts like twin milkfed / fawns and lids over eyes / like twin clouds' evoke the Song of Solomon. Gibbs's allusiveness to other poets encompasses echoes of Eliot's *Four Quartets* near the end of 'The Road from Here,' his 'Homage to Neruda', two poems for Ralph Gustafson, and his adoption as titles of his poems quotations from William Carlos Williams ('to imitate nature involves the verb'), Roberts ('Not in the flower but effort toward the flower'), and Wallace Stevens ('His soil is man's intelligence').

While Gibbs is a poet of phenomenal physicality – of crickets and grasshoppers, doves and finches, burdocks and beggarticks – he's also a poet of dreams and fantasies, of 'chimerical dancers', 'some astral anti-bear', and a 'raven wind' that declares 'I am that bird that eats up / death itself'. In one of his poems, a kitchen clock escapes into the night; in another, a poem of visionary ecological devastation and hope (phrases from the Book of Revelation not too far away), the poet sees 'the ends of the world' yet also hears a voice shout '*Tierra tierra*' (again, this time in Spanish, *Earth*). Two of his most fascinating narrative-driven longer poems not included here, 'Events Underground' and 'My First Second Coming', establish fantasies or dreamscapes where the laws of waking consciousness are suspended, but also where the dreamer's fears and perplexities are connected to fears and perplexities in the waking world.

Robert Gibbs's poems first appeared in print in 1950, but he worked at his craft, studied and taught poetry, and developed his amalgam of styles over many years before publishing his first chapbook in 1968 and his first full-length collection two years later. The full range of Gibbs's development requires attention to his poetry of the 1950s, the majority of it published in *The Fiddlehead* (I've located twenty-nine of his poems in that journal from between 1950 and 1960, and another ten from 1960–66; none of these poems appeared in either his first chapbook or first long collection, though some were reprinted in *Five New Brunswick Poets*, a 1962 anthology in which he shared space with Elizabeth Brewster, Fred Cogswell, Alden Nowlan and Kay Smith). This short volume of poems selected more than half a century after Gibbs began publishing poetry is not the place for an exploration of how his poems changed between 1950 and the most intense period of his poetry-publishing (1968–78); for now I'll merely note that his early poems tended to be more conventional in their versification and 'literary' in their language, and less personal, humorous and flexible with lines and stanzaic patterns, than the work of his middle and later years.

Picking poems for this book was arduous at times due to the wealth of possible choices, and I found it painful leaving out poems that have dazzled, delighted and moved me. Gibbs's strongest poems are among the most distinctive of the past half century in Canadian poetry. The bountiful body of his sharp-eyed, muscular, humane poetry needs a much wider readership on its journeys 'skipping round the biosphere'.

— BRIAN BARTLETT

An Untimed Instant

Light trims the white edges of the bay,
Limestone licked clean by salt-loving tongues;
Light determines the angles of the cliffs
And ciphers the incalculable long division
Of the tides. Light accounts all dimensions,
Carries its unknowns to highest powers
And final roots. Light polishes lens
And prism to catch an image of the utmost
Depth. Where light hails white on the shallow
Flats, dry air is quickened thick
With wings beating upward into heaven.

In such a radiant counterpoise,
An untimed instant, a herring school is netted,
Dense silver bellies half held to the light,
And quick mother-of-pearl skins wet wounds
Left by ebbing tide over the web of rock and pool.
Light waters the sea, solving thick-tongued thirst,
Breaks the salty crust of tideline, washes
The cry of seabird and ticking clock
Of the tide into a shining stillness.
White, white supersaturation!
Even the still wind is quieted
Caught in the rigging of the sun.

Now, one by one, seeded into the eye,
Rhomboid and pyramid, prism and sphere,
Red, green and yellow the crystal angels
Ascend, descend, singing until
Light itself is flooded and immersed
In sky, rock and tide breaking out.

The Road from Here

I

The road from here to Saint's Rest
    takes you by the asylum farm
    a set-design for *Oliver Twist*
    swings and slatted benches in the yard
    for the mindless bones of old ones
    who laugh you by toothlessly
    on to Saint's Rest.
And for the slow beginners farther on
    giving a kind of headstart
    a fresh yellow hospital school
    on a government stamped landscape
    usurps our rock cranberry patches.
The way to Saint's Rest
    has graveyards right and left
    Protestant and Catholic
    both seawashed
    with baywind-bitten stones.
Beyond the beach canteen and radio towers
    the road to Saint's Rest peters out
    to stumbling blocks of blackened stone
    (odd Victorian ends of curlicue and gargoyle
    from the old twin-towered customs house
    razed now and replaced
    by a more customary and unbedevilled concrete box).
The path to Saint's Rest
    along the cliff edge
    and sometimes off the edge
    takes you round Smuggler's Cove
    a hellmouth inaccessible except by water
    doubtless now the best
    and only certain way.

On my walks from here
    I turn my back on it
    knowing how west it is
    around the coves
    and the unhoppable gaps
    I make for it a longer way.

II

From here it is no easy walk away
    without foot benefits
    of seabird-feathered sea-ribbed sand.
Some internal fire
    has compoted mud and granite
    into purple puddingstone
    or garlic-stuffed peppercorned
    pink Polish sausage.
Walking here's a boulder hopping
    or crabwise scrabbling back
    out of sole-breaking slippery clefts
    where tide-ends slicker over slime.
Sometimes on top
    room enough for one foot
    to drop the other
    and tread air
    allows glances out
    where sheet lightnings shake the offing.
The groaner often turns me back
    sucking its breath
    from some inward spasm of the bay's sickness
    off Partridge Island.

III

The roads and we that take the roads
    come round to this –
Will the end itself
    ball up the ways
    it takes to get there
    and swallow all?
Or will even the sea spew up
    conglomerates?
A paved road through woods
    spreads a banquet table
    redfox, skunk and crushed porcupine
    for unsettling crows' craws.
Here and there squares of green
    wedge into walls
    for old men to poke through litter baskets
    after yesterday's news.
Fresh blood on the sand
    sets another table in the wilderness
    sweetmeats for vultures.
Ragged marches
    all the young in arms
    flag hate with love.
Signs, signs everywhere advertise
    graveyards for every conceivable death
    and parish houses for every conceivable madness.

IV

I know how the stones will be
 when I get there
 (taking the Chichestrian way)
 salt-white in sun
 and milled smooth as marbles
 ungarbled in the mouth
 of the lapidary ocean
 yet not done
 as nothing stone is done
 until it is sand
 and nothing sand is done
 until it is dust
 and nothing dust
 till so dispensed in light
 as to become light.

The roads and we that take the roads
 (with us as we must)
 become ourselves in going out.

Transmigrations in the Five Worlds

Ch'ien-feng asked, 'What kind of eyes do they
have who have transmigrated in the five worlds?'

A Cheshire cat's not for swinging
that spends all its fat self
becoming a grin without a mouth
or any poem that says it wants to be
a song without words.
My words should have the grace
                    to hop off the page
like the frog in the Scotchman's porridge
                    as clean as they came.
By the time you've caught this by the tail
                    and swung it round and round
more than likely you'll agree.

Reading these koan of the masters
I think I hear a little
                    as much through nose as anywhere
the solid music of the unhollowed
                    hallowed iron flute
                    the kind of carol
Alice might have heard
where time is never beat
and standing still keeps you
                    running fast
on both feet.

I find myself wanting to clap
western-style with both hands
saying how little of their grace I've taken
though my eyes stuff my nose with sweetness
as I watch from inside
a Chinese-looking girl
stooped with string
in thick mist taking
into her own head
                    and slenderness
                    the droop from dripping
full fleshed peonies.

The Death of My Father

My father died Christmas Eve in
the middle of the night and
the green breath of the big tree
in our frontroom mixed with
the dark smell of death upstairs.
My mother called us in and said
'I think he's gone, your father's gone', and
seeing the slack black gape
of his mouth, I thought of the cold
bluebodied turkey in the fridge downstairs.

A praiseworthy man, on Sundays out to meeting
with praise of God in his eyes and not
a pigeon missed with breadcrumbs nor
a dickybird in the gutter and not
a tomcat passed with his ruff
unruffled or his rough purr unpurred.
A man simple enough, in love with sunsets
and butter-and-eggs by the railway tracks
where we took our Sunday walks around
the waterfronts and afterwards reformed
baptist hymns which his thick fingers pressed
from the thick strings of his cello.

I see you dad, on your high stool in
your shop, eyeglass wrenched into play and
fine curly gold turning up and off from
your keen engraver as you cut 'Love for
always and always' on the inside circus
of a secondhand wedding ring.
And how we hoarded the dust from
every sweeping in a tall black can and
shipped it away to the refiner to have
your gold and silver letters, all
your days' cuttings from coffin plates
and baby spoons, cradled out
in his white secret fire and
sent back, sent back.

All Such Movements

I see the fairground lights
scrambler tilt-a-whirl and ferris wheels
make cosmic rings
with imaginary poles
to chase bears around
and keeping all their greasy mechanical necessities
to themselves
except by day

I see my father's big thumb turn
winding our old kitchen clock's two springs
on Saturday night
mistrusting its claim to be good for eight days
and wanting in any case
to keep his sabbath free from time's necessities
its catarrhal gong
bangs off the hours and half-hours
of twenty-five-odd years
its gilt pendulum swinging
behind the window of its gingerbread cage

All such movements are
as precise and settled now
as my cleanly compassed horoscope
cast by a cool-eyed poet
unflinching
in its conjunctions and oppositions
Things don't need to show their works
but some do
like our four-hundred-day clock
whose wheels on wheels
carried on a Ptolemaic universe
of gold-plated brass
under a crystal dome

So things go on or might

for eight or fifty times as many days
          if one night
the mirror over our mantel hadn't shattered down
          with a nightmare-rending crash
          on our crystal clock
          and if that were not enough
some days later our kitchen clock
          broke out clanging
off the hour
          taking off across the night
like a runaway from a carousel
          tearing up the air
with free and shivering apprehensions

Skipping Round the Biosphere

Whatever the lighthouse means   flaring round
            off-beat with the foghorn
making its connections and disconnections
            in this watery envelope
where black-backed gulls work their wings
            indifferently it seems
in either element   and the herring weir
            makes thin lines and crosses
a Japanese virtue or virtuosity of restraint
            where crows in a tough row of willows
mark the tide's edge by out-hoarsing
            the gulls
and rotten dulse and salt steam through
            musk of steeplebush
and wildrose perfume   and spruces on the point
have their backs bridled up for good
            against all winds

Whatever three ships mean
            two freighters and a tanker
            standing off Partridge Island
more like scanned-for presences
            than anything really out there
(I saw three ships come sailing in
            come sailing in   singing itself
            off-season   off-key)
Whatever the fine grading means
of every weight of gravel by the tides
            coarse and round at the edge
an even band of sand between and broken flak
            up to the tideline

Whatever the whole watery egg means
            that holds a half-hatched world
ready to crack at the sun's first tinny glint
            and spread itself

an instant peacock's tail of clear distinctions
        eyes and things to see
is not of my making
        but more like putting down
most of what I see or want to see
        and what I don't
(caught in fog with my ballpoint skipping)
        in invisible ink

'His Soil Is Man's Intelligence'

for Molly Bobak

The blueberries bluest fat and thick
sun-heated most and double sweetened
disordering overgrown tops of family graves
I never picked for the pail
not wanting to answer for an unfamiliar
familiar taste in my mother's pies

But when I wanted to
with a special hunger for the sun's bluest
soft-skinned heat
I ate them greedily
pulled off in bunches and tumbled straight in
purpling my teeth

with a sweetness munched out of sweetness
and made a dark tongue for myself
to leer with
out of my overripe fathers' royal clustering

For a Sketch of Lovers by Bruno Bobak

In this embrace
I can see no acting
this rounding of body on body
fingers through fingers
no thing more sudden
in coming or going
than growing
his sinews bowing round
her years to fashion her
as they are now
scruff of bark on tough heartwood.

And in their eyes see
no attending
where none is needed
both sets bent off
as if on long gone sufferings
carried here
separate yet mutual
each knowing each.
I see long roads falling back
streaming with brothers
mothers, handcarts and bundles.
Their eyes peak up
like nodes of barbed wire.

This repose is gnarled
as roots clean exposed
naked
showing all the scars of growing
under ground.

'To Imitate Nature Involves the Verb'

Nahamee of the Squamish
struck out this head
with an unwavering blade
and this must be his own face
flashed here
and known as a man knows his own
from looking out of it
not at it

And when he freed himself
he cut loose the tree
disclosing every ridge of grain
known only to itself
His fingers rubbed themselves out
setting his wood's assertion
against his own features
the marks he made on it

What a sharp selfhood
he must have brought
to his cutting edge
to uncover them both here
his own and the wood's
You'd have to handle this
unsmiling head yourself
to know how man and tree
secure each other

Old Man Whelpley

You hadn't reached your ninetieth year
    or taken your third wife
    when I knew you best
    saintly in your white whiskers
    rocking on your verandah
    in Beulah Campground
    where whitewashed stones
    spelled out in black
    shouts of the redeemed seldom heard
    and a sign on the beach said
    NO SUNDAY BATHING PERMITTED

Your blue eyes steadied behind their glasses
    as they took in the seven-mile measure of the Reach
    and you spoke heretically to one
    you thought might understand
    not of retribution
    in or out of a mad God's hands
    but of restoration
    your breath crowded with hosannas
    as your eyes sang the words they saw
                                        far off
    THE RESTORATION OF ALL THINGS

Even the devil? the boy couldn't help asking
Even the devil – you said.

From *A Dog in a Dream*

I: i

Clock   ding a dong
nighthawk   shriek your shriek
across a line of flying
that calls for your note
over Crow Mountain

Bay   salt a flood moon
slopping up the slips
take stairs one by one
bob fishing boats about
masts   straighten up to catch slant glints

Dark   face back out of the way
leave dreams blind and inflame
stringtied lovers
and nighthawk wings' white darts
tear a night well rounded

II: iii

What to see inside
are jelly cells set
to serve and save each other
passing light along
ruby to ruby
polarizing and refracting
and letting in shadows here and there
of Pluto's black gold and chariot wheels
that nothing can keep out

Even honeycomb and pomegranates
having strong-sided walls
to keep each cell from each

(every seed its own tree inside)
never chance
two without one, shake without tremble
and inside themselves
their bright sweet lights
must figure jointedly and indivisible

II. iv

It was no dream
I saw a poet flounder on a river
sticky and black as mimeograph ink
I saw him blooded
and eaten off
Leeches jerked like typewriter works
digging salt from his hair roots

sugar from his tongue
Words no longer words
divided him asunder
and left him to stink
like a split fish on a drying rack
a kipper
an unread herring

III. i

To get out as you got in
the direction as things are
is past understanding

It might be burrowing
using hands as forepaws
mounding dirt between your haunches

Far enough in pucker your lips
and think of tree roots
pulling the earth's dugs

That is the bottom of the stairs
the root cellar where sprouty-eyed
Irish spuds know which way to look

The very bottom or you might
without reversing say the top
and feel underfoot a stair

twisting the other way
an anti-stair so to speak
down from there

and its bottom like all bottoms
when you get down to it
past understanding

Up these three stairs or down
like looking up a coatsleeve
I think I see stars

burn out in showers
with no excess behind
losing none and gaining none

The old equation
energy is understanding
but there is that

past speaking of
that blocks chinks between words
however much they sputter up

III. ii

Paddy McGaughey played the bones
between his fingers
on Bridge Street April Fool's Day
at three o'clock in the morning
and whooped and danced a Donegal jig
while his pockets jingled
and his double-looped watch chain
snapped across his belly

and all us kids clapped out the windows
till our mothers smacked our bums
back to bed
The moon that night coloured Irish whiskey
lit the seven skinned eels
hung to dry in Perdad O'Reilley's boatshed
and there were dreams crossing dreams
all over Indiantown

IV: iii

The frogs are singing now
light as cattail fur
            blowing off
last year's rushes
unbuzzy and soft as algae

From gold eyes and sprouts
            deep down
you can hear baby Moses
being lullabyed this minute
into an Egyptian sleep

Our own daytime divers
charm into frogs and what airs
must tickle their nostrils as they say
            The Primal
is what we're after

flippering bits of slime mould
from their eyes
but they'll spring back gaping
            the bends
fizzing through their fancy blood

drunk to display their deepest finds
bottles stoppered still
            from Pharaoh's time
They'll wave rubber arms
in amphoric euphoria

Rapture of the Deeps
for proof foolproof
of princes primary to frogs
            glad to know
the green selves they've lost

VII: v

If I could split free
of forethought and afterthought
I'd make lawless noises

of love with no measures
taking out stitches
in all that seems seamed

but severing is ours
day to day and month to month
toward this peaking year's midnoon

where brides measure veils
against morning sun on bedroom walls
like daisies sighted in tall timothy

and who will keep one from that tapping
on her window light as snow
from His year's midnight His day St. Lucie's

IX. i

I will come down out of my tree house
wingless
shinnying   clawing at gum
scraping the sides of my knees

I will come down and walk old Slapfoot
that gives spring for spring
and tumbles back its dead
namesake of that Micmac traitor

smacking along it still with tendons cut
I'll meet eyes-on
and give and take
what passes here as love but has no name

where nothing sticks
and spottedness cuts spottedness
to greens beyond words
as lightnings auger down

I will advance as far as the far pools
where gold-eyed frogs coil
springs in pea-sized brains
and meet halfway the shapes

that press against my misshaping tongue
Whatever I've shed will sustain
where in the last pool
a gold well unwellable

I see the coiled snake dragon-deep
rounding out the blocks
of a mosaic wall consume
flickers of chimerical dancers

* * *

To touch like this in sleep
foot to foot and elbow
to elbow passes in trust
all waking holds

A Kind of Wakefulness

You've left no door or I'd knock
you sacked in your silk house
bug   worm   whatever you are
so there's no getting in or I'd come
and wrap myself in your fine suspense
breathing as the earth breathes
once or twice a winter

Maybe it's a way of getting wings
to spread in a big spring show

slowing down that much
taking winter for what it is

these days when the westerlies
shake teeth loose
and needle eyelids through
as if to stitch them up

Or I'd join a bear in dreams
exchanging my spirit maybe
with some astral anti-bear
who'd amble the night sky wide awake
while my head joined numb ground
under a heaved-up stump
in a fellow heaviness

dreaming likely
of green caves under the sun
where in August heat raspberry canes
bent together
light their cool spaces
with heavy sweet combed fruit

Dreaming what the earth dreams
breathing to its bass
must be a kind of wakefulness
sharper-eyed
than this fleeced and muffleheaded
snow blindness

Depth of Field

Through my camera's dead set
you come clear yet some ways vaguer
than those trees behind you
yellowing silver poplars out of focus

Pinned to my long eye
matched line to line across a hairsbreadth
you're losing sight for me and touch
lengthening armslengths

And at my dark eye's end
I've lit this ikon limned wholly
in blue and gold outside my own kind
or yours of seeing and being

What cheer is there in making it –
you – a Eurydice girl who went
underground too soon
and passed beyond blackness

way out in front?
Beautiful? Yes, more than ever
by any hard standard
fixed that way

composing a ghost, no two
laying them I'll say
by settling our love
bodydeep in outside ground

'Not in the flower but effort toward the flower'

(at the old Brewster place, Hammtown on the Washademoak)

With a head so full of old houses
nested one inside the other
and holes gnawed between
for rats to squeak through
or bats to keep chittering apart
one more   yours
shouldn't matter

It had a way of being there
when we couldn't see it
looming out of the woods
and standing its ground
as if its piece of sky and lakeshore
thorntrees down to mudpacked rocks
were cut away for it

Sometimes with all my houses stuffed inside
I feel roofless
leery of summer storms and lightning bugs

Walking in through raspberry tangles
past the collapsed verandah roof
we knew we'd find layers of paper
peeling from scabby plaster
and all the refuse a last tenant leaves
the mildewed copybook grade 4
with its kid's bear story
and upstairs the rusty mattress
overhanging its bedframe
coming unstuffed

And dust enough to catch
light from the front dormer
but none of it human

The imprint we looked for
wasn't there
though you made it being there
and will
make it again and again
carrying in your head all you need
to steady its sills
and bend its rooftree straight

Sometimes I think myself of changing houses
feeling beams sag and joists heave
and hearing sharper angles of wind
whistle down my rocky flue

When we looked for the pool
and the flagbed
it was there deep and cool enough
though dry
with mud hard as its stones

But you brought it water
and called into sight
its shot-eyed flower

Conservation Procedures

A fire spirit humps and troubles
here and there
running from the centre outward
then breaks in foaming spit
like a red pulse breached
The jelly pot's aboil

Highbush cranberry juice
dripped and squeezed from a cotton bag
lights round the fulmination
as if the sun were in it

forecasting maybe
a January one that will so shine
through flattened clusters ruby-red
left for it and winter birds

Pith scums and cruds yellow grey
and the skimming spoon clears it
like coating from a tongue
whose buds for tasting bitterness
sugar down and drown
in clarified syrup

But what a thickening power
must be in it all
waiting out this troubling heat
to pull the cells round
into rosettes and tetrahedrons
of crystal jelly

Cranberry flesh conserved
to stand in bottles on a window sill
turning all its summer out
in sweet blood light

A Summer Composition

The brightest flower in all my garden is
that red canoe   water-shaped and hand-shaped
antipodal on its sawhorses under the white
birch   Even so it carries

summer's full load   bobbing
righted to its rightful steam
These diggings made for late seeds
and seedlings readymade are dutybound

to decompose like any grounds for summer
not least that rich intermingled bird
music made out of registers each
has to keep himself between tunes

like those dances everyone knows
he must do alone or not dance
at all   So this composition
where the eye's led to glance off

red   that red canoe   poppy-coloured
(or blood   glanced at another way)
this composition comes down the page
as the steps do   to the weathered

picnic table and the rhubarb gone
to seed and the turned-over earth
dry at its edges   down to me
batting through bugs and maintains

its wavery line between all
unwavery lines decomposing it
and back to a blooming
made by hand to float

Aubade for Bad Dreams

It runs on all night   that strange music
windy old horns and squeezeboxes
sackbuts and serpents   leathern sounds

When a violin crooks my elbow
I find myself playing Go Down Moses
in grand E-minor chords

All this after my rocktop study with its
sleek tables and typewriters
shelves booked to the ceiling and candles

on stands repeated in the great glass wall
over the valley   I'm looking back
at that grand interior surprised to see

how small its lights burn
Off the muddy path I'm smothering
in last year's goldenrod

I pull myself up by quarter inches
and stubbed nails   All this
and after such dreams that morning star

hanging so near it looks to be
closer than the backyard elms
and that topped-over new moon

flawed in the cracking creek in
haystubble ice   splinters a million ways
Air they float on   all that ice

that moon   that star   that small east
queezes and wheezes making up all the
Lord God Almighty lights of a March morning

From Morning Songs

20

for Desmond Pacey

My eyes ran along that compass
watching so intently they pulled
my arms outward after them
wanting to enclose what it
enclosed

Look   look   I said   here it must turn
here it must encircle
those who've danced in the Spirit
all night long
shakers and quakers
foolish saints half transported already
These surely are the objects of its grace

Seeing further on
those who'd sweated and prayed
under stormy lamps
days and days longer   I said
Look at that company set loose
on all the roads
Here it must shut in
the very children of its mercy

But its bent was always outward
straightening against all curvature
till my arms ached after it
and my throat choked on
the low-strung cry of its love
that would not
cut inward to cut out
a single blade of grass
or feather fallen from one bird

All This Night Long

All this night long and longer
I've been taking inventory of
country roads   and sometimes less
than roads   tracks and logging ruts and
blazes all but healed over
all the ways of getting from the centre
of this woods to that point
along the shore   that place where
a light beams out and a horn
thickens through inblowing fog

All of them over rough tracks past
raw slashes and green newgreen in
burntover humus and blueberry patches

Sometimes after a single man
on foot   along rivers and off them
up steep brooks   seeing him step
round or jump over logs and stumps
into staghorn moss or wild mushrooms

Seeing him break his way or wade
long enough to know the motions
he makes with his head and hands
cocking ears at a birdcall or
stooping over a pebblebed for one
to turn in his hand   or toss
two or three times   before giving
it back with a giving all his own

In and out of counties   across
borders   through swamps and flooded-out
intervals   slogging all night long to
make connections more connected   to say

See how it all radiates   or how
it all assembles   to say
Hey you there   insisting you are
there   Hey I have you here

And that gentle plodder   parting
many thicknesses   is no more apart
from you than you from me

From Everyman Jack

I

Littlejohn Tow tramping the dockyards
caught a Liverpudlian cold from a tart
in a Merseyside house   wished himself
home in Lincolnshire eating suet
pudding from his mam's hand or selling
bullseyes to nippers in his dad's shop

Littlejohn Tow shipped out on a countess
a cow-carrying steamer   as deckhand
and counted the waves one by one
all the way to Kingston Jamaica

Littlejohn Tow lost in a Fundy fog
and a dozen odd saloons after lying
a fortnight in quarantine off
Partridge Island   jumped ship and
rolled off to the lumberwoods
back of Hillsborough to earn
his keep   marry a Steeves   and scratch
enough dirt up Nixon way to feed
a brood of kids and plymouth rocks

Littlejohn Tow now in Sunday blue
stays behind on the church steps
one of the brethren and blows his nose
heartily as unto the Lord

2

He didn't know if he shouldn't or should
Her back was long and her knees were good
And the breath of her   her breath
Was like sweetmouth apples

He didn't know if he durst or durn't
He did think though   it's time I learnt
The taste of her   her taste
Like January apples

'Boys O boys I'm gone to town
This time' he said 'she'll have a youn
A boy like me   like me a boy
A pippin Johnny apple'

3

Bunion-footed John pilgrim
bounded over his county hills
while bound in a dream in a Bedford
gaol and fell upon sloughs
and dragons and the topside

of that bottomless bottom
Abounding in grace he rounded
the shape of it that hump
his untollable weight and bent
under it like any manjack

Vanities and lights of heaven
batwide wings that whisked
his face caught in such a dream
are leaves from an old book
engraved in steel against time

5

Ah Presbyter   slick mottled
salamander squirting from my hand
back to your mud   slime of slimes
uncongealed slippering through

cold as ice as death   wintering
through summer   uncrackled   slickering
doublequick through fiery
Heracleitos' brain

You keep your phoenix skin shut
to half opened eyes   your grin
fixed that way to snap
skipping shadowgraphs   these

fixities you laugh at
Your murky socket you turn
inside out making your dark
shine doubly dark   You

cast all black as white
moist as hot earth as air
the pit as paradise
you make of old Plato

a cold potato
Swoooooook   Squeeeet
Hold on a minute   Am I
even half through with you?

7

John of Patmos' eyes
light over what's gone
on what's to come
lock like mandibles
a mantis' or a rhinoceros beetle's

on a new green leaf
But your words my grandfather
John   great grandfather
John   great great John
are vocal whisperings

of birds flying together
that turn on edge
with no back or forward
dimensions go out
and on like thin lights

John (what John was that?)
saw tender joints
where a horned beetle joins
and a black wasp pierces
saw a blue mole nose his way

through goldthread roots
saw light piercing
out of stone
unrocking granites
Does love   this love

concentrate or dissipate?
John   goldentowned John
catchall of bright scatterings
closes his book
sealed and all ready

From Verse Journal

I

East of here the first riser
out of this dark has made
a light   a fire   a prayer
of some kind   has looked
his way for first signs
and this way for last

has breathed the first air
off the Atlantic   tasted
the first salt   and felt
the tide's pull before it
unscrambles in his loosening
earbones

Someone should take down
his innocence while it's still
unbiled by any aftertaste
of forgiven things   or foretaste
of things to be forborne
Someone should register

as on a map or seachart one
might a beacon his
singularity and the unstudied
praise he makes making his first
cup of tea before his mouth
has soured on a word

Someone should look to
the sleepers he kisses
lightly enough to leave
in sleep   when he says
Well
I best be going

5

Gang way   someone shouts and
drays and slovens lumber
down our street heaped with
corn husks and goat dung

Gang way for the beasts   and
drovers goad bellowing cows
all bells and the great black bull
dragged along by his ring

A fancy-dress general with pips
and ribbons   tries a goosestep and
follow-the-leader antics for kids
who wave banners and scatter

leaves   crazy with their high
stepping and that Salvation Army
major's old drum drum drum
keeps his dead march alive

from his knees to his elbows while
his belly ploughs forward and his
Onward Christian Soldiers crosses
Tipperary and warhorse marches

coming the other way and all
night long that old Yankee whispers
If you want to compound interest on
your foolishness   keep it strong

6

That grace I would return to
curved against my sleeping form
arms caught together and legs
and breasts like twin milkfed
fawns and lids over eyes
like twin clouds over quicksilver

That grace   that mould of me
making of me one true thing
whole as a bellied whale-shape
white fits another black
to make all seven seas
round on their sphere

That grace   that roundedness
warm and generating warmth
flowing in and out of itself
wheel against wheel shedding
sparks and sheets of light
thundering heat and bursts of rain

That grace   that sleep
so well opposed to my waking
I withdraw from
stealthily and whisper
Wait   wait a little
till I break this perfect egg

10

Out of that black northwest
on a long wing blacker
than itself
the raven wind comes flying and crying
its sad black cry

Everything it touches
chills and blackens
the very air under its
one long wing careering whistles
to its cry

I am that carrion bird   it says
that bitter wind
I am that bird that eats up
death itself
I harden all sluices

block all slush and skim
crude scum   dipping down one-sided
on your plate   Let me
lick it clean   Let me be
the death of you

you dead thing
you yesterday

20

That is a horse I hear
breaking into the night
a riderless horse coming

at a good clop up
our street   churning winter
dust enough to leave
pools of diffuse moon
light   What is that
horse?   What is that
horse doing out so
late with no reins
or rider? Passed now

I hear him still
breaking the unbroken song
Is that he whinnying
so far now away
he sounds like the bleat
of a newborn lamb?
a lamb with silk ears
bleating and taking milk
from his mother for the first time?
It is already morning and
sparrows begin keeping faith
with it   song sparrows

who portend nothing
portentous   Then the redwings
stabbing through
the black dog's bark
as he too wants
to get in on the start
But what can make that echo
pass wholly out of range?
What laughter can unchoke
a throat's silence?
And what hawk bids
for fury in that sky?

Nocturne

What am I doing out here in the night
under a hard moon?   I say it to myself

What am I doing here with a torn blanket
and a frayed bedspread covering collapsed vines

hairy summer strongmen that are the first
to go? Maybe a night or two of killer frosts

will give way to slippage   a mellow
retraction   Keatsian mist to round summer out

But what a wishful country tune
I'm singing as I give this grey old CN blanket

motheaten someone stashed in my attic
another flip to catch tomato stakes

Silver leaves already on their backs
make their own frost spots

as the toughtalking firmament
claims half and more than half

Who Asked Me to Be a Reader of Entrails?

He asked me what the signs were of late
spring a hot summer dearth
I said I could not tell though they
were all around I was sure

He asked me where I'd look Was there
an almanac of sorts or did we have our own
Old Indian I said there must be
one of each from what I'd heard

He asked if there were still new moons
fish days fasts on the drugstore
calendar Were the wormcasts heavier
than usual? The sun warped

one side or the other? Did the river
stink more pungently? The eels
slide out of it deliberately? Who
had laid the woodchuck on his side

in such a deep remission? Were the ravens
racketeering in glossier encopements? Why
did the sky blacken again without
intention? I had no answer and told him so

I who scarcely know my right hand from
my left Who asked me to be a reader
of entrails or unraveller of dreams?
He pointed to the earth He pointed to the sky

He called the moon bloody and so it was
He stopped on my threshold and would not
come in took sips of tea outside but refused
meat wasted As for me

what would I do when winter days came on?
I would keep my two ears warm unnip
my nose and muffle my feet I would walk
around my neighbourhood with no falls

The Keeper's Keeper

Your name I cannot recall   It sleeps
somewhere in my lowest-energy cells
lit with no light at all   forgotten

as anything is forgotten   shadow of a name
wobbling along some slack nerveway
Those lost syllables might have kept

you alive and more than that me   kept
love   but something resisted and has
gone on resisting   Don't forget too

what wanted it put by and kept there
something active maybe in the name
itself   some fatness like that

a sleeping groundhog feeds on   Dragging
it up now like a bag of dead kittens
would be bad enough but finding it

still powered to shine from inside
might be that much worse like knowing
right out loud who is the keeper's keeper

This Catching of Breath at the Top

I hear a clock strike   a hammer
hammering   and a robin's urgings
I hear my own breath in this breathless

standstill   this midsummer dark
lit from inside every
dripping leaf   The pine outside

my window's wick'd with new
ten-to-twelve-inch wicks
Ten marigold lamps light the

sprout-beds   set there to
set back the resident groundhog
Fog and drizzle pace all

breathing to a vegetable speed
Standoffs   arrests   stalemates   infest
inaudible and invisible currents and cross

currents   those unstoppable warbles no
warbler at his or her business
pays attention to   After

today I know which way my
garden will turn   I know how soon
in all this green liquefaction

I'll taste oxalic needles
This catching of breath at the top
is like the catching of breath

at the bottom   a turn in the dance
I live in   and live by   one that
will go on turning after every

clock in the house has struck and
every carpenter has hammered every
nail   fast   home

Hale-Bopp Syndrome

This little river has carved
a canyon for itself to snake through
down to an outlet under the fence

where it cascades into snow-sponge
Generations of frost laid down
through storms and thaws of this

latest ice age   hold unnibbled
by the sun that plays peekaboo
with the northwest corner   It will take

a lot of weeping to make a heartbeat
quiver in this stone   It will take
more than one penitential

psalm streaming back from the comet
overhead to free these doors to shut
and open   Finches twitterfill the air

and chickadees practise lovenotes
one falling off another
sadly   I must exit gingerly

at first light tomorrow   I must
forestall garbled bassoons   goosenotes
with my own broken calls

A Post-Christmas Carol

In the bleak widwinter   choirboys sing
voices as untainted as snowflakes on a swing

I like to think of shelter for all that friendly crew
and the child as lowly   ox and ass and ewe

dumb before the shearer   tough to whip and goad
born to do the carrying   not to be the load

Even snooty camels have to learn to kneel
before high-crowned magi can try out their skill

News comes on of horses that stumble out-of-doors
eleven down-country   leavings from old wars

Their shelter makeshift   ribbed   like their sides
nose to nose they nicker   lice in their hides

their dead half-buried or dragged to the woods
breakfast for foxes   supper for their broods

Why all this outcry? someone justly frowns
Children go as hungry right in our towns

earth stood hard as iron   chills more than cheers
no quick fixes and no going shares

A stall and some fodder   a pat on the nose
all a beast asks for to make it nuzzle close

The beadle's friendly wisemen designate shelves
where kids without voices will live inside themselves

Why all the outcry? Because they are dumb
They'll freeze uncomplaining till someone finds them room

Snow has fallen   *snow on snow*   Will coldness never end?
and Guernica's broken critters find a way to mend?

Alden-and-Robbie's Day

25 January

When winter stays in place cold and white
under pine-needles under snow
the shrew lives out her January Doves
scatter and tail-over-head squirrels
skitter blue on the perfect yard Shrew
noses out of her tunnel gingerly as an angel
to lip a sunflower seed and slip back

Maybe she has babies in there to pull
on her nailpoint nipples How much
deeper in her bunker she has to hunker
in these days of January thaw before
the wind turns back to his proper quarter
and snuffs improper green with whitestuff
Today in particular meeting-place

of two poets' birthdays so wide
apart yet nearer to each other each
time they happen Alden-and-Robbie's day
Peculiar it should be so dark this noon
crepuscular a half-poet might call it a
louring glowering sky yet not un-
befitting two born to lopsided days

and nights two who warmed themselves
and us with hot brews and distillates who
died both early withdrawn from us yet
as much here as the shrew's nose
that pokes out quivering over and over
questing questioning whatever light there is
to take from it her winter bread

From 1492 / 1992

2

Our great globe floated in the atmosphere of infinite space
like an insubstantial bubble. – Nathaniel Hawthorne

I saw a light like a little wax candle
rising and falling   I heard a wind sift
through pine needles like a fine rain
Then my spirit left my body as a moth

leaves its broken house in the dark and goes
spellbound toward a lantern hung from a mast
a spirit out of the night flying to where
the bent world turns round below it

I saw the green of a green place sicken and
pale past yellow into grey   The sun's
red eye opening over the edge
singed trees of weeping habit and

scorched lizards belly-up   Cries
caked together from nests and nestlings
flamed and shrivelled   I saw boulders
grind their teeth and all the icecaps

weep   I was there at the ends of the world
Then I heard someone shout *Tierra tierra*
and I knew that the globe of my body was there
where I left it and my voyagings not done

The Irishness of Summer

The green sides of daylight are sides
of a stone   an emerald   May's stone
or Mary's   kept into summer   hard

burning summer   Seven shades
of green   a prism's worth my eye
looks into as into a leaded

window and down into a crypt
lit with apocalyptic lights that will
call worms out of holes

chicks out of nests   songs
out of throats branded and
choked   but freed   let loose by the

Irishness of summer   its wolfhound
keenings and holy mawkishness
Under all this green

red   bedded in   waits
its turn to answer   the way an organ
answers calls to prayer by gorging

on the air pumped into it   Red
will masticate all this in its time
the woods bonedry as they are   but green

will keep its own three-leafed
evangel   against the kicks and pricks
of wasps and leggy hoppers

About the Author

Robert Gibbs's paternal great-grandfather was a Gibb from Kenneway, Scotland, who served in the navy and later settled in the Midlands of England; after the move, 's' was added to the family name. The poet Gibbs's maternal ancestry (Towers, MacQuarries and Hoars) stemmed from Scottish and Irish roots. When she was a young woman his mother, Bessie Tower, from Turtle Creek, Albert County, New Brunswick, spent two years in Saskatchewan. There she worked as a cook for a threshing crew and turned down a marriage proposal, then returned to the Maritimes in 1925. She soon regretted the move and hoped to return to Moose Jaw, but then she met Robson Gibbs, an engraver and jeweller, and married him in 1926. Her third son, Robert John Gibbs, was born in Saint John on February 3, 1930.

After early schooling in Saint John, Gibbs furthered his education at the University of New Brunswick in Fredericton and at Cambridge University, where he was an IODE Scholar from 1952 to 1954. At UNB he completed an MA thesis, 'Symbolism and Imagery in the Poetry of T.S. Eliot'. For several years he taught in his native province. In 1950 Gibbs's poems began to appear in *The Fiddlehead*, and during his years of taking classes and studying for his first two university degrees, then working in public schools, he was one of the contributors whose work appeared most frequently in that journal. One of his professors at UNB, clearly an influence on his writing, was the brilliant polymath, poet and cultural historian A.G. Bailey, whose life and works Gibbs would honour over fifty years later in his poem 'AGB'.

The many-faceted Protestantism of Gibbs's family had an impact on his imagination in both poetry and fiction. His father was raised Anglican, and his mother Baptist. The great aunts and uncles among the MacQuarries (his mother's maternal line) included Bliss, a grocer at whose house Robson Gibbs boarded when he met Bessie, and a Reformed Baptist who later became a Pentecostal minister. Aunt Flo was a Seventh Day Adventist, Uncle Charlie a Wesleyan, Aunt Sadie United Church, Uncle John a Christian Scientist on PEI, and Uncle Cliff – a potato farmer in Carleton county – a Jehovah's Witness. Even though Gibbs's mother would tell him that he inherited his 'gift of gab' from the MacQuarries' maternal line, the Hoars, actually it was the spirited religious loyalties of the MacQuarries themselves that inspired some of the drama, comedy and colour in his two collections of short fiction, *I've Always Felt Sorry for Decimals* and *Angels Watch Do Keep*, books which revolve around Hutchie and Pompman Killam, the orphaned children of missionaries.

In 1963 Gibbs began his many years of service teaching at UNB. In his spare time he began working on a doctorate, which he completed in 1970 with the dissertation 'A Study of Irony in the Poems of E.J. Pratt'. He held various administrative positions in the Department of English, including Director of Creative Writing and of Graduate Studies, and worked in several editorial capacities for *The Fiddlehead* from 1968 until after his retirement in 1989. Eighteen years after his first publication of poetry in literary journals, Gibbs's first chapbook, *The Road from Here*, was released in 1968 as the first of the New Brunswick Chapbooks series, followed two years later by his first full-length collection, *Earth Charms Heard So Early*, published by Fiddlehead Poetry Books who also published Gibbs's subsequent collections during the 1970s, *A Kind of Wakefulness* and *All This Night Long*. The community workshop 'McCord Hall' or 'The Icehouse Gang' on the UNB campus provided the first audience for many of his compositions during the 1970s and '80s, and Gibbs offered insightful criticism and generous support for many other writers there; it was also at McCord Hall that he began reading aloud his Hutchie and Pompman stories.

When he was fifty-five years old, Goose Lane Editions published a new and selected poems by Gibbs. Oberon Press of Ottawa published his books of short stories, as well as his two novels *A Mouthorgan for Angels* and *Kindly Light* and two volumes he edited of Alden Nowlan's newspaper columns for *The Telegraph-Journal*. As Nowlan's literary executor, Gibbs also edited a volume of the poet's new and selected poems for Irwin Publishing. Though Nowlan is nationally and internationally better known than Gibbs, diligent readers will want to explore the similarities between these two Maritime poets as well as their considerable differences. Gibbs's poetry possesses both the intensity and the originality required to inspire and influence Canadian poets and those of other countries now in the twenty-first century.

Robert Gibbs: A Bibliography

POETRY

The Road from Here (chapbook) (1968)
Earth Charms Heard So Early (1970)
A Dog in a Dream (chapbook) (1971)
A Kind of Wakefulness (1973)
All This Night Long (1978)
The Tongue Still Dances: Poems New and Selected (1985)
Earth Aches (chapbook) (1991)
Driving to Our Edge (2003)

STORY COLLECTIONS

I've Always Felt Sorry for Decimals (1978)
Angels Do Watch Keep (1997)

NOVELS

A Mouthorgan for Angels (1984)
Kindly Light (2007)

BOOKS EDITED

Ninety Seasons: Modern Poems of the Maritimes (with Robert Cockburn) (1974)
An Exchange of Gifts: Poems New and Selected, by Alden Nowlan (1996)
White Madness, newspaper columns by Alden Nowlan (1996)
Road Dancers, newspaper columns by Alden Nowlan (1999)